PIANO • VOCAL • GUITAR

She's got the BLUES

ISBN 0-7935-1557-2

Hal Leonard Publishing Corporation

7777 West Bluemound Road P.O. Box 13819 Milwaukee, WI 53213

PIANO · VOCAL · GUITAR

BLUES
She's got the

CONTENTS

AFTER YOU'VE GONE

By CREAMER & LAYTON

BABY, WON'T YOU PLEASE COME HOME

Medium bounce tempo

Words and Music by CHARLES WARFIELD
and CLARENCE WILLIAMS

I've got the blues, I feel so lone - ly, I'd give the world if

I could on - ly make you un - der - stand. It sure - ly would be

grand. I'm goin' to tel - e - graph you ba - by,

BABY WHAT YOU WANT ME TO DO

By JIMMY REED

Moderately slow

1 You got me run-nin'   You got me hid-in'   You got me
2   up,   Go-in' down,   Go-in'
3 peep-in'   Got me hid-in'   Got me

run, hide, hide, run,   a-ny way you wan-na, let it roll____
up, down, down, up,   a-ny way you wan-na, let it roll____
peep, hide, hide, peep,   a-ny way you wan-na, let it roll____

BASIN STREET BLUES

Words and Music by
SPENCER WILLIAMS

BILLIE'S BLUES (I LOVE MY MAN)

By BILLIE HOLIDAY

CRAZY BLUES

Words and Music by
PERRY BRADFORD

MCA music publishing

DON'T EXPLAIN

Words and Music by BILLIE HOLIDAY
and ARTHUR HERZOG

DOWN HEARTED BLUES

Words by ALBERTA HUNTER
Music by LOVIE AUSTIN

days.
hand.

It seems that trou-ble's going to fol-low me to my grave.
Going to hold it, ba-by, till you come un-der my com - mand.

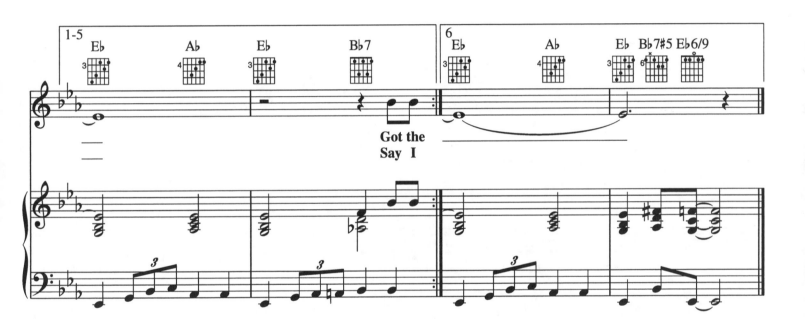

Got the
Say I

Additional Choruses (Ad lib.)

Chorus 3:
Say, I ain't never loved but three { men / women } in my life.

No, I ain't never loved but three { men / women } in my life,

'Twas my { father, brother / mother, sister } and the { man / woman } who wrecked my life.

Chorus 4:

'Cause { he / she } mistreated me and { he / she } drove me from { his / her } door,

Ye, { he / she } mistreated me and { he / she } drove me from { his / her } door,

But the Good Book says you'll reap just what you sow.

Chorus 5:
Oh, it may be a week and it may be a month or two,
Yes, it may be a week and it may be a month or two,
But the day you quit me honey, it's coming home to you.

Chorus 6:
Oh, I walked the floor and I wrung my hands and cried,
Yes, I walked the floor and I wrung my hands and cried,
Had the down hearted blues and couldn't be satisfied.

DON'T GET AROUND MUCH ANYMORE

Words and Music by BOB RUSSELL
and DUKE ELLINGTON

EVERYDAY
(I HAVE THE BLUES)

By PETER CHATMAN

loves me, no - bod - y seems to ___ care; ___

Speak - in' of bad luck and trou - ble, well, you know I've had my ___

share. ___ I'm gon - na pack my suit - case, ___

___ mov - in' on down the line, ___ oh, ___

FINE AND MELLOW

Words and Music by
BILLIE HOLIDAY

Moderato

My man don't love me, Treats me Oh so mean, My

man (he) don't love me, Treats me aw - ful mean.__ He's the

low-est man That I've ev-er seen. He wears

high draped pants_ Stripes are real-ly yel - low;_____ He wears

high draped pants_ Stripes are real-ly yel - low. But when he

starts in to love me He's so fine and mel-low._____ Love will

make you drink and gam-ble, Make you stay out all night long,_ Love will

47

FEVER

Words and Music by JOHN DAVENPORT
and EDDIE COOLEY

you all know. Fe - ver is - n't such a new thing,

fe - ver start - ed long___ a - go. burn.

Verse 3 Romeo loved Juliet
Juliet she felt the same,
When he put his arms around her, he said,
"Julie, baby you're my flame."

Chorus Thou givest fever, when we kisseth
Fever with my flaming youth,
Fever – I'm afire
Fever, yea I burn forsooth.

Verse 4 Captain Smith and Pocahantas
Had a very mad affair,
When her Daddy tried to kill him, she said,
"Daddy-o don't you dare."

Chorus Give me fever, with his kisses,
Fever when he holds me tight.
Fever – I'm his Missus
Oh Daddy won't you treat him right.

Verse 5 Now you've listened to my story
Here's the point that I have made:
Chicks were born to give you fever
Be it fahrenheit or centigrade.

Chorus They give you fever when you kiss them,
Fever if you live and learn.
Fever – till you sizzle
What a lovely way to burn.

GULF COAST BLUES

Words and Music by
CLARENCE WILLIAMS

GLOOMY SUNDAY

Words and Music by SAM LEWIS
and REZSO SERESS

Death is no dream, for in death I'm ca-ress-ing you. With the last breath of my soul I'll be bless-ing you.

Gloom-y Sun-day! Dream-ing, _____ I was on-ly

dream-ing, _____ I wake and I find you a-

sleep in the deep of my heart, dear. Dream-ing, _____

A GOOD MAN IS HARD TO FIND

Words and Music by
EDDIE GREEN

Lyrics:

My heart's sad ___ and I am all for-lorn, ___ my man's treat - ing me mean. ___ I re-gret ___ the day that I was born ___ and that man of mine I've ev - er seen. My

HEAR ME TALKIN' TO YA

Words and Music by
LOUIS ARMSTRONG

MCA music publishing

HOLD WHAT YOU'VE GOT

By JOE TEX

You had bet-ter ___ hold ___ on,
(See additional lyrics)

hold on to what you've ___ got. ___

You had bet-ter ___ hold ___ on, hold on to what you've

Additional Lyrics

Recitation
Listen fellows, you know it's not all the time that a man can have a good woman,
A woman that he can call his very own; a woman who'll stay right there at
   home and mind the children while he's gone to work.
A woman who'll have his dinner cooked when he comes home.
Where some men make mistakes is when they go out and stay
   because they feel that no other man wants his woman but him.
Well, listen...

Chorus 2
If you think no other man wants her,
Just throw her away and you will see
Some man will have her
Before you can count one, two, three.
Yes, he will, yes, he will.

Recitation
Listen girls, this goes for you, too, because you know I've seen so many women
   who've had so many good men in life,
Men who'd stand by them through thick and thin, men who'd go to work every day
   and bring home their hard-earned pay;
Men who'd give their women anything that their little hearts desired.
Where some women make mistakes is when their men let them go out and play,
And they stay, because she felt no other woman wanted him but her.
Well, listen...

Chorus 3
If you think that no other woman wants him,
Just pitch him out in the street and you will see
Some woman will have your man
Before you can count one, two, three.
Yes, she will, yes, she will.

I ALMOST LOST MY MIND

Words and Music by
IVORY JOE HUNTER

I CRIED FOR YOU

Word and Music by ARTHUR FREED,
GUS ARNHEIM and ABE LYMAN

I WILL NOT BE DENIED

Words and Music by
JERRY L. WILLIAMS

Lyrics:
1. The true love sto-ry is
2.,3.,4. *(See additional lyrics)*

hard to find. Can't get no rest, got no peace of mind.

They say you gave your heart to me. You put me down and

76

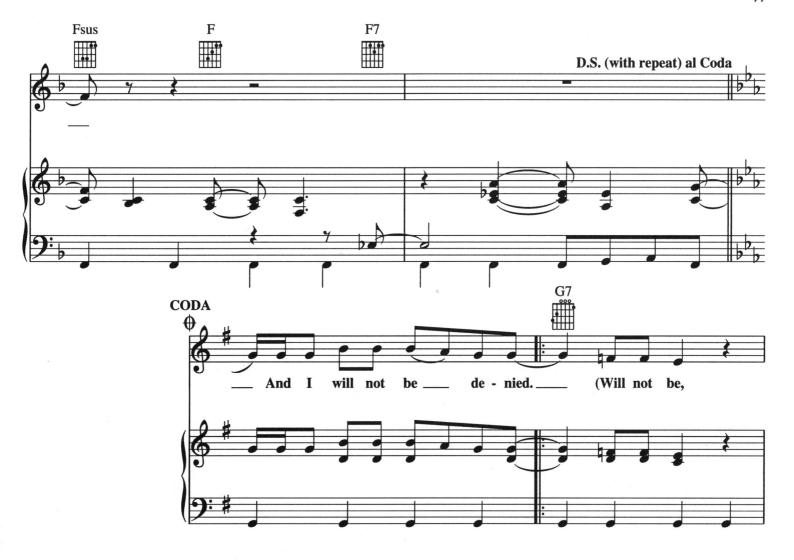

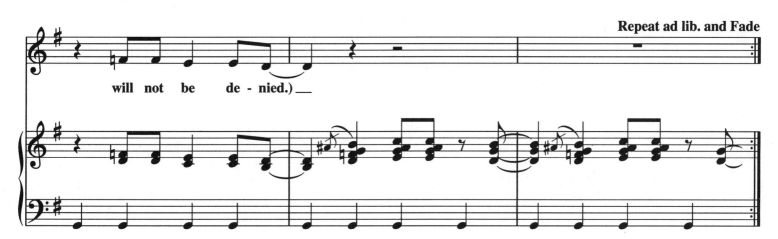

Additional Lyrics

2. **You said you were the only one.**
   Come in on me and ruin my fun.
   Leave me sittin' at home all alone.
   Waitin' on your call by the telephone.
   To Chorus

3. ***Instrumental***
   To Chorus

4. **It's a sad situation, yes, it's true.**
   I can say it, baby, I'm through with you.
   It's over now and in the past.
   Gonna find me a man with a love that'll last.
   To Chorus

I'M A WOMAN

By ELLAS McDANIEL
and KOKO TAYLOR

(Spoken:)

I can wash out forty-four pairs of socks and have them hangin' out on the line,
I can rub and scrub till this old house is shinin' like a dime,
If you come to me sickly, you know I'm gonna make you well,
I can stretch a greenback dollar bill from here to kingdom come,

I can starch and iron two dozen shirts before you can count from one to nine,
Feed the baby, grease the car and powder my face at the same time,
If you come to me hexed up, you know I'm gonna break the spell,
I can play the numbers,   pay my bills,   and still end up with some.

I can scoop up a great big dipper full of lard from the drippin's can,
Get all dressed up, go out and swing till four a.m. and then
If you come to me hungry, you know I'm gonna fill you full o' grits,
I got a twenty dollar gold piece says there ain't nothin' I can't do.

Throw it in the skillet, go out and do my shopping and be back before it melts in the pan,
Lay down at five, jump up at six and start all over again,
If it's lovin' you're lackin', I'll kiss you and give you the shiverin' fits,
I can make a dress out of a feed bag and I can make a man out of you,

(Sung:)
'Cause I'm a

wom-an, _____ Dou-ble u o m a n. (Spoken:) I'll say it a-

gain. gain. (Sung:) 'Cause I'm a wom - an,

Dou-ble u o m a n. (Spoken:) And that's all.

I AIN'T GOT NOBODY
(AND NOBODY CARES FOR ME)

Words by ROGER GRAHAM
Music by SPENCER WILLIAMS

JAILHOUSE BLUES

Words and Music by BESSIE SMITH
and CLARENCE WILLIAMS

(Spoken:) Lord this house is gonna get raided! Yes, sir!

Additional Lyrics

2. You better stop your man from ticklin' me under my chin, under my chin,
   You better stop your man from ticklin' me under my chin,
   'Cause if he keep on ticklin' I'm sure gonna take him on in.

3. Good mornin' blues, blues how do you do? How do you do?
   Good mornin' blues, blues how do you do?
   Well, I just come here to have a few words with you.

THE JEALOUS KIND

By ROBERT CHARLES GUIDRY

THE LADY SINGS THE BLUES

Lyric by WILLIAM ENGVICK
Music by ALEC WILDER

The la-dy _____ sings the blues, the la-dy _____ walks a-lone, she's got no dream at all, _ the heart she used to call _ her own _____ has turned to stone. _ The

MAD ABOUT HIM, SAD WITHOUT HIM, HOW CAN I BE GLAD WITHOUT HIM BLUES

Key of C (C-Eb)

Words and Music by LARRY MARKES
and DICK CHARLES

*Symbols for Guitar, Diagrams for Ukulele.

LONG GONE BLUES

By BILLIE HOLIDAY

Oh tell me, ba-by, Tell me what's the mat-ter now? Tell me, ba-by, What's the mat-ter now? Are you try-in' to quit me, ba-by,— But you don't know

LOVE ME OR LEAVE ME

Lyric by GUS KAHN
Music by WALTER DONALDSON

LOVER MAN
(OH, WHERE CAN YOU BE?)

by JIMMY DAVIS, ROGER "RAM" RAMIREZ
and JIMMY SHERMAN

pray'r that you'll make love to me, strange as it seems,

some day we'll meet and you'll dry all my tears, ___ then whis-per sweet lit - tle

things in my ears, ___ hug-gin' and a kiss - in', oh what we've been miss - in'

lov - er man, oh where can you be? be?

THE MAN THAT GOT AWAY

(From The Motion Picture "A STAR IS BORN")

Music by HAROLD ARLEN
Lyric by IRA GERSHWIN

MEAN TO ME

Word s and Music by
FRED E. AHLERT and ROY TURK

MY HANDY MAN AIN'T HANDY NO MORE

Music by ANDY RAZAF
Lyrics by EUBIE BLAKE

Once I used to brag a-bout my han-dy man __ But I ain't brag-gin' no

MY MAN BLUES

Words and Music by
BESSIE SMITH

121

I guess we got to have him on ___ co-op-er-a-tion plan. ___

(Clara:Spoken:) **Bes-sie!** (Bessie:) **Cla-ra!** (Both:Sung:) **Ain't noth-in' dif-f'rent**

'bout that rot-ten two ___ time man.

Dialogue II

Dialogue I
(Bessie:) Is that you, honey?
(Charlie:) Tain't nobody but—Who's back here?
(Clara:) It sounds like Charlie.
(Bessie:) It is my man, sweet papa Charlie Gray.
(Clara:) Your man? How do you git that way?
(Bessie:) Now, look here, honey, I been had that man for umpteen year.
(Clara:) Child, didn't I turn your damper down?
(Bessie:) Yes, Clara, and I've cut you every way but loose!
(Clara:) Well, you might as well be get it fixed.
(Bessie:) Well, then…

Dialogue II
(Bessie:) How about it?
(Clara:) Suits me!
(Bessie:) Suits me! Well, then.....!!!!

NOBODY KNOWS YOU WHEN YOU'RE DOWN AND OUT

Words and Music by
JIMMY COX

PINK BEDROOM

Words and Music by
JOHN HIATT

Moderately Fast Rock

She paints her fin-ger nails___ for-bid-den tones,___
She thinks all her boy___ friends are so dumb,___
They say they got her fu-ture down at the desk,___

she wants ner-vous youth___ on the tel-e-phone.___
she drinks Co-ca Co-la with her val-i-um.___
now they're draw-ing blood___ for the grown-up test.___

her pink bed - room.

PLEASE HELP ME GET HIM OFF MY MIND

Words and Music by
BESSIE SMITH

Additional Lyrics

2. I've come to see you gypsy, beggin' on my bended knees,
   I've come to see you gypsy, beggin' on my bended knees,
   That man's put something on me, oh take it off of me, please.

3. It starts at my forehead and goes clean down to my toes.
   It starts at my forehead and goes clean down to my toes.
   Oh, how I'm sufferin' gypsy, nobody but the good Lawd knows.

4. Gypsy, don't hurt him, fix him for me one more time,
   Oh, don't hurt him gypsy, fix him for me one more time.
   Just make him love me, but, please mam, take him off my mind.

RIVERSIDE BLUES

Words and Music by THOMAS A. DORSEY
and RICHARD M. JONES

SAN FRANCISCO BAY BLUES

Words and Music by
JESSE FULLER

Mean-while in an-oth-er cit - y, Just a-bout to go in-sane,__

Seems like I heard my Ba-by, The way she used to call my name,__ If she

ev-er comes back to stay, There's gon-na be an-oth-er brand new day__

Walk-in' with my Ba - by down by the San Fran-cis - co Bay.__

SEE SEE RIDER

Words and Music by
MA RAINEY

SENTIMENTAL JOURNEY

Words and Music by BUD GREEN,
LES BROWN and BEN HOMER

SOME OF THESE DAYS

Words and Music by
SHELTON BROOKS

SOME OTHER SPRING

By ARTHUR HERZOG, JR.
and IRENE KITCHINGS

SORROWFUL BLUES

Words and Music by
BESSIE SMITH

With a blues feel

Additional Lyrics

2. I got nineteen men and won't want more;
   I got nineteen men and won't want more.
   If I had one more I'd let that nineteen go.

3. I'm gonna tell you, Daddy, like Solomon told the Jew;
   I'm gonna tell you, Daddy, like Solomon told the Jew.
   If you don't likee me, I sure don't likee you.

4. It's hard to love another woman's man;
   It's hard to love another woman's man.
   You can't catch him when you want him, you got to
      catch him when you can.

5. Have you ever seen a preacher throw a sweet potato pie?
   Have you ever seen a preacher throw a sweet potato pie?
   Just step in my backyard and taste a piece of mine.

SPOONFUL

Words and Music by
WILLIE DIXON

Medium beat

1. It could be a spoon-ful of dia-monds,
could be a spoon-ful of cof-fee,
could be a spoon-ful of wa-ter,

Could be a spoon-ful of gold.
Could be a spoon-ful of tea.
Saved from the des-ert sand.

Just a lit-tle spoon of your
Just a lit-tle spoon of your
But one spoon of them

pre-cious love___ sat-is-fies___ my soul.
pre-cious love___ is good e-nough___ for me.
for-ty fives___ saved you from an-oth-er man.

Men

lies_____ a - bout it, Some of them cries_____ a - bout it,

Some of them dies_____ a - bout it,

Ev-'ry - thing__ fights a - bout a spoon - ful, That spoon, that spoon, that spoon.

1. 2.

3.

2. It
3. It

ST. LOUIS BLUES

Words and Music by
W.C. HANDY

161

Extra Choruses (optional)

Lawd, a blonde-headed woman makes a good man leave the town,
I said a blonde-headed woman makes a good man leave the town,
But a red-head woman makes a boy slap his papa down.

O ashes to ashes and dust to dust,
I said ashes to ashes and dust to dust,
If my blues don't get you my jazzing must.

STRANGE FRUIT

Words and Music by
LEWIS ALLAN

STORMY WEATHER
(KEEPS RAININ' ALL THE TIME)

Lyrics by TED KOEHLER
Music by HAROLD ARLEN

'TAIN'T NOBODY'S BIZ-NESS IF I DO

Words and Music by PORTER GRAINGER
and EVERETT ROBBINS

THIS BITTER EARTH

By CLYDE OTIS

TROUBLE IN MIND

Words and Music by
RICHARD M. JONES

MCA music publishing

two nine - teen__ ease my trou - bled mind.__

Trou-ble in mind, I'm blue,__ But I

won't be blue al - ways, 'cause that wind's gon - na come__ and

blow my blues__ a - way.____

TROUBLE IS A MAN

Words and Music by
ALEC WILDER

I had a vi-sion of love _____ and it was all that you've giv-en to

me. _____ I had a vi-sion of love _____ and it was all _____

no chord

that you turned out ___ to be, _____

WANG DANG DOODLE

By WILLIE DIXON

1. Tell Au - to - mat - ic Slim, ___ tell
Crawl - in' Red, ___ tell

Ra - zor Tot - in' Jim. ___ Tell Butch - er Knife Tot - in' An -
Ab - ys - sin - ian Ned. ___ Go tell ol' ___ Pis - tol Pete, _

- nie, tell Fast Talk - in' Fan - nie.
to tell ev - 'ry - bod - y he meets, to -

194

Additional Lyrics

3. **Tell Fats and Washboard Sam that everybody gon' jam.**
   Tell Shakin' Boxcar Joe, we got sawdust on the flo'.
   Tell Peg and Caroline Din', we gonna have a heck of a time.
   And when the fish scent fills the air, there'll be snuff juice everywhere.
   To Chorus

WHEN THE SUN COMES OUT

Lyrics by TED KOEHLER
Music by HAROLD ARLEN

WOMAN ALONE WITH THE BLUES

Words and Music by
WILLARD ROBISON

YELLOW DOG BLUES

Words and Music by
W.C. HANDY

E'er since Miss Su - san John-son lost her Jock-ey, Lee, __ there has been
I know the Yel-low Dog Dis - trict like a book, __ in-deed I